9 to 9

The Life of a Car Salesman

Dedication

This book is dedicated to the memory of…

My father, Allan "Bubba" Berman. I always miss you, Dad.

Nat "Pop Pop" Kellman, who loved and cared for my mother for 30 years.

My grandparents, Buck and Marie Berman.

My maternal grandparents, Joe and Reba Schwartzman.

My Aunt Sheila.

My wife's parents, Phil and Dorothy Saba.

I've kept my promise, sir.

Contents

Introduction

Remember when you were young and your parents asked, "What do you want to be when you grow up?" I'm sure your answer wasn't, "A car salesman!" You probably replied with something like, "I want to be a doctor!" Or, "A policeman!" Maybe you wanted to be a fireman or even a lawyer.

I wasn't any different. I either wanted to be a doctor or a lawyer like my father. Never once did the thought of selling cars come to my mind. As with most people who got into the business, it was an accident. You may know or may have known someone in the business. You may have seen an ad for automobile employment somewhere. Car dealers are good advertisers and they're even better at getting you hooked on their ad.

However, it is never really planned. If you were told what the job entails, you would not have pursued that kind of employment. If they were honest with you upfront and told you all of the hours that you had to work, the family time that you're going to miss, the beratings, and not to mention all the rejection from the customers, you would've surely picked another profession.

What they do tell you upfront is that you can make a lot of money. They point out the one guy in the dealership that has it all figured out and is doing very well. You think to yourself, *if he can do it, so can I*. What they don't tell you, is of the 100's of others that came before and tried and failed. They don't point out the ones that are there now not making a living because it's totally commission.

In the upcoming pages, I will introduce you to just some of the ins and outs and daily activities that I have experienced in the automobile industry. I hope to show you that not all car salesmen and managers are created equal. We are not all bad.

With big eyes, an open mind, a ton of ambition, and even more naivety, this is my story of how by chance, I got into the business of selling cars over 30 years ago.

Chapter 1
The Title

"Hey, what's the schedule?" I asked someone at the dealership as I was wandering around aimlessly during one of my first days in the business.

"You're on the B shift," he replied without hesitation.

"The B shift...what's the B shift?"

"You'll figure it out," he said as he walked away.

He was right. It didn't take long to figure out that *The B Shift* meant that you were to be there when they turned the lights on, and you better be there when they turned the lights off.

Most retail businesses open up at 9 AM. Car dealerships aren't much different, so I thought. Most dealerships open up at 9 AM and close at 9 PM. Most are Monday through Friday 9 to 9, and Saturday 9 to 6. It depends on the dealer. Some dealers are open until 7 PM on Saturdays. They do that just to one-up their competition. The dealer with the biggest ego, who won't be outdone by anybody else, his dealership is open 6 days a week, 9 to 9.

Sundays are determined by the dealer and the blue laws. Thankfully, the county that I worked in did not allow car dealers to be open on Sundays. I never understood how the malls could be open on Sundays but the car dealers could not. They are both retail businesses. I didn't question it though. I was just happy to have a day off. So why did we have to work

9 to 9? Why was I put on the B shift? I soon learned the answers to these questions. Let's start with the incompetence of the sales managers. For one, I don't think they know how to make a schedule. Scheduling takes time and competence. Neither of which they had.

Secondly, we are paid strictly on commission and could miss out on a sale if we weren't there bell to bell. You can't predict when a customer will come in and ask for you. It would not be uncommon if a customer came in and asked for you while you weren't there, and whomever in the store greeted that customer says to them, "Oh I'm sorry, he doesn't work here anymore. I'll be happy to take care of you." I know what you're thinking. How could they do that? What if the customer comes back in and found out their original salesperson is in fact still working there? The managers didn't care. They couldn't be bothered. They were too busy. And too incompetent.

It is really embarrassing when a customer you waited on says, "Oh I thought you didn't work here anymore. I bought my car from so-and-so." You can't get mad at the customer. It's not their fault. And the salesman isn't going to get in trouble with the managers because he sold a car. That's all they care about.

So I learned early on, you better be at the dealership. Call it what you want. The B shift, bell to bell, ding to dong, open to close, or simply: 9 to 9.

I also worked in a market where it seemed like the employees in the sales department competed to see who could work the most hours. Just because the hours on the front door say that we close at 9 PM, that doesn't mean that we get to leave at 9 PM. What if there is a late deal? There is no leaving. You have to make every deal.

If a customer walks in at 8 or 8:30 pm and wants to buy a car, you do the math. It takes three hours to buy a car - minimum. That's if everything goes right, which rarely happens. The worst is starting a deal late, you go through the whole process, and it's now 11:30 PM. You've been there since 9 AM and what do you know? The deal doesn't go. For a number of reasons, it didn't happen. Often times it was the customer's credit or lack thereof. What bank do you know of that's open until midnight? Not one in the area of our dealership. Maybe the customer was unrealistic about what they could afford, or it just simply took that long to find out you were not going to be able to agree on numbers. Maybe you couldn't verify insurance. And forget about getting the car cleaned for delivery that late if the deal was a go. So now your 12-hour shift just turned into a 15-hour day. It's getting toward the end of the week, and you've got 75 hours under your belt; we haven't gotten to Saturday yet. Saturday is a whole different animal in itself. Saturday is the busiest day of the week for 6-day-per-week car dealerships. Most people are off on Saturdays but not car salespeople. Saturdays are forbidden to take off. The dealership could double or triple their week's sales with a successful Saturday.

And don't forget about the Saturday morning meeting. Be early on Saturdays to get pumped up and motivated before the customers roll in. Whether the meeting was at 8 or 8:30 AM, it just added hours onto the already long work week. I learned another way of the trade early on: don't be late for the Saturday morning meeting. If the door was unlocked and you walked in late, be prepared to be embarrassed. Picture this, a guy walks in late, and the meeting stops. Everyone looks at him, then they all begin to clap and laugh. Then the manager moderating the meeting says, "Thanks for interrupting my meeting. Now go out and wait for me in my office. I'll have a special meeting just for you." Saturday's morning meeting was supposed to be upbeat, a time to get everyone excited to have the best day of the week, a time to give out spiffs to get the guys going. Monday morning meetings were the beat-down meetings.

Saturday seemed easier because we were busier, and like in life, time really flies when you're busy. In another way, they were easier because we knew going in that we were scheduled for a nine-hour day rather than twelve. I can tell you that in over 30 years of being in the car business, and 30 years of Saturdays, I can count on one hand the amount of Saturdays I left at or around 6 PM. Now, your *easy* nine-hour Saturday just spiked to 10, 11, or 12 hours. Add that to the 70+

hours from Monday to Friday: we will be approaching about 90 hours for the week. Luckily for me, it didn't matter what time I left on Saturday nights because I knew I'd be off on Sunday. Most guys didn't love giving up their Saturday nights, but they chose the car business.

I felt for the guys working in the *'open-Sunday'* market. Working in a *Sunday store*, you could work 100 hours or more in your week. I often weighed the importance of everything. The hours, the beatings, the rejection. Was it worth it? Was it enough money to give up everything else? I watched guys compete over hours. The question was, how long could they do that for? I could not and would not work 90 hours a week. I was closer to 70-couple hours a week. I looked at it as working half of a day; or 12 of the 24 hours. If you look at it that way, 9 to 9 is only half of a day of work.

Chapter 2
How It All Began

It was in the year 1982 when I was working at a small Ma and Pa pizzeria. Now, this is not just any pizza shop. It's the best in our small Maryland town. We not only had the best pizza but we also had the best subs. Imagine this: we sold the best pizza in town by the pie or by the slice!

You have to remember that this was before Papa John's, Domino's, and Pizza Hut. Needless to say, we were busy. It was a hangout for the teenagers and a family place for dinner. I had been working there throughout high school, graduated in '77, and continued slinging pizzas at Mike's into my early 20's. To put it simply, I was working pretty hard and going nowhere fast. Mike's was so busy that I was going in and working the lunch shift before my actual shift even started. This was my introduction to *half-a-day* workdays.

At this point, I wanted more. It was time to grow up and start thinking about the future. I started reading the classifieds in the Sunday paper, every Sunday. Again, 1982: before LinkedIn, Monster...Google. I searched every weekend - but for what, I really didn't know. I was just tired of not making real money and going home with flour in places flour should never be.

Like I said, we had the best pizza. We made it all by hand right there in that little shop. We would toss the dough in the air to make a thin pizza. We got really good at it. Sundays were our busiest nights. It was pretty clear that no one in town cooked dinner on Sunday nights. We put on a show with spinning the dough. We probably made between 150 and 200 pizzas during the three-hour dinner rush. Add in the sub orders, the carry out customers and the phones ringing; it was something to see. What a well-oiled machine we were. We all had a job to do.

Back to the classifieds. One job I accepted was to sell signs to businesses. Door-to-door. Wow, did I get sold a bill of goods. No salary, all commission, and the training - there wasn't any. Good luck. Needless to say, that didn't last more than a day.

Then there was an ad that caught my eye.

`"Own your own pizza shop. Training Included."`

Now, this is me. I can own my own business. And it's a pizza shop!

I called right away. The guy on the other end seemed as excited as I was. He said that I was the perfect candidate. That's what I thought too. He went on to explain that this new company has revolutionized the way to make great pizza. And get this: they figured out a way to do it faster than anyone else, and delivered *hot* within 30 minutes. Their business model was to locate their shops near college campuses so that they could deliver a lot of pizzas to one place at the same time. He told me this new company was called Domino's.

I was in. I was told I would have to relocate to one of their stores and go through a manager-in-training program. Once I passed their course, I could get my own store. That sounded great to me. Just like all the other ads I answered. Like the one to sell carpet. I don't know what possessed me to try this out. I guess I'm a sucker for these no-salary jobs where they hire as many people as they can and hope one or two of them make it. Once I found out that they were selling second, third, and fourth run carpet, I was done there.

The closest Domino's was a few hours north off Interstate 95 in Rutgers, New Jersey. I found a room to rent in someone's house for $50 a week. With everything I owned packed in my backpack and duffle, I took a leap of faith and headed up 95 in my 12-year-old POS. How I found the house that had my new room was a miracle in itself. Remember, 1982: no iPhones, no MapQuest, no Waze.

The very next day I started my career at Domino's. I found the store (somehow again, no iPhone). Looking back on it, the fact that I found the house and the Domino's store is truly amazing. It's hard to get anywhere nowadays without my phone navigating me. Back to Domino's. I walked in, and the manager was there to see me. He told me they were busy and could really use my help. I knew I could handle a busy pizza shop. Let's get started.

It was really the same process as the one we had at Mike's. The difference was this place was brand new. It was as modern as you could get for the time. It was easy. Their process took me all of 10 minutes to learn. I mean, how hard is it to put the sauce on the dough, the cheese next, and then the pepperoni? Once the manager was comfortable with me up front running the store, I didn't see him much after that.

A few weeks went by. At this point I'm out of money, my car barely runs, and I'm no better off than I was at home. So I called the guy who hired me for the ad.

"I'm ready for my own store!"

"Okay. I need you to go to one more location for us and help them out. We can talk about your own store later."

They sent me to New Haven, Connecticut. This particular Domino's was located there to serve Yale University. I remember pulling up to the store in the afternoon - pure daylight. I saw the light on and people working inside. I walked up to the door, pulled the handle, and it was locked.

The guy behind the counter buzzed me in. Mike's certainly didn't have a door buzz.

"Why's the door locked? It's the middle of the afternoon."

"This isn't the safest neighborhood, man."

What? I couldn't believe any of this. They sent me to an unsafe neighborhood, where they deliver pizzas *while* carrying cash. I couldn't believe all of this was going on so close to the campus of Yale, of all schools.

I used their landline to call the corporate office. I let them know that there was no way I would work in that environment. I asked for what was in the ad: My own pizza shop.

Finally, I got a person who read the fine print to me.

In order to own a franchise, you need a lot of money.

I don't remember the exact amount. But it was around $100,000 - up front. I could barely afford a room for $50 a week in the basement of a stranger's house.

That was the end of that. Now I'm back in New Jersey, watching TV, wondering what would be next. As I'm flipping through the 8 channels offered, a commercial comes on for the United States Navy. The Navy had the best commercials on TV at the time.

It's not just a job; it's an adventure. See the world.

So what else does a young man do, broke, busted, and disgusted? He goes down to the local recruiting office and joins the military.

I took an entrance exam that seemed to take all day. The man I handed my test to, graded it right on the spot.

Then he said, "Go ahead, pick what you want to do in the Navy."

Some of the options offered, I would've had to go to somewhere cold for boot camp. I was born at night but not last night. So I picked a school where boot camp would be in a warm place. Well, it was November, what would you do? There was really no reason to make this any harder than it was going to be. With all that being said and done, they gave me a date for the following week.

"Next week when you show up, you'll sign up officially, and we'll tell you when you'll ship out."

Perfect, I thought. *I can make my buddy's bachelor party back home this weekend.*

Heading south on 95 my POS decides to break down. Perfect timing. I somehow hitched a ride the rest of the way, and I was on time to meet everyone at the first of many bars for the evening. Since this was going to be my last weekend of freedom before joining the Navy, I proceeded to get very drunk. It didn't take much for me because I never really drank. Not even back then. I never acquired a taste for alcohol. But it seemed like the thing to do that Saturday night at the bachelor party.

I don't remember which bar it was when one of the guys in the group started talking to me. I didn't know who he was. After a few beers, I'm talking to this stranger about the Navy, how broke I am. I told him that for the next four years I'm just going to see the world and everything will be paid for by the Navy. I was just going to cop out. I was going to put everything I made in the bank. What would I need money for? They feed you, clothe you, and provide accomodations. Perfect right?

I guess I gave him a chance to speak because next thing I know he's telling me about what he does. He sold cars. Actually, he was a sales manager at a dealership.

"Hey, why don't you come sell cars with us?"

After a laugh, I thank him and tell him I'm going to see the world while serving in the Navy.

"Listen, if you can speak this well when you're drunk, you can sell cars."

"Thanks man, but I'm going to raise my right hand and join the Navy next week."

"You can join the Navy any time. Come sell cars with us. If you don't like it, then go join the Navy."

He was right; at that time you could join the military anytime you wanted to.

"Okay, you got me thinking. But I have a couple questions."

He's waiting to hear them.

"Well, you guys wear suits and ties, right?"

"Yes, we do."

"I don't have any suits. All I have are jeans and t-shirts."

"Don't worry. I'll buy you a couple of suits and a couple of ties. You can pay me back next month when you get paid."

"You'll do that? We just met."

"Sure I will."

"Okay, well what about food? I really don't have any money left."

"Again, nothing to worry about. I'll buy you lunch and dinner at McDonald's for the next month. When you get paid next month, you can buy me lunch and dinner."

"Okay, what is this next month thing?"

"That's how we get paid - once a month. You'll get used to it."

"Got it. Last thing. My car broke down on the way down here. I don't have any transportation."

"Again, no problem. We'll give you a brand new car to drive. Everyone gets a demo to drive."

I was thinking all of this over in my head. *Let me get this straight.* This guy is going to buy me a couple of suits? Correct. He's going to buy me lunch and dinner for a month? That is also correct. And he's going to give me a brand new car to drive? Absolutely. *Well, then how can I say no to all of that?*

"When and where do I begin?"

"9 AM Monday morning."

Chapter 3
Green Pea

Whether you're a customer or an employee, it's pretty intimidating to walk into a car dealership. First of all, the dealerships themselves are usually huge, uninviting structures. Secondly, you never know what to expect when you walk in. So, you can imagine what I was feeling at 9 AM Monday morning when I walked in those big front doors.

No one talks to you. They didn't even say hello to me. Finally, someone directed me to my new friend. He seemed happy to see me.

"Let's go get you some proper attire."

We walked across the street to the 1980's version of Men's Wearhouse. It was an enormous place with tons of suits and everything else a man could possibly need for his wardrobe. The gentleman who helped us knew exactly what I needed. A dark blue suit. The first staple of every man's closet should be a dark blue suit. It probably shouldn't be 100% polyester like my first suit was.

The suit salesman said, "Good news. This suit comes with two pairs of slacks. One pair is dark blue, and the other pair is beige. The sport coat is dark blue so, *voila!* You now have two suits. Oh yeah, it also comes with a vest. The best part of the vest is that it's double-sided. One side is blue, and the other side is beige. So now, not only do you have two suits, you have two, three-piece suits."

Two white shirts and two ties later, I'm ready to start my career as a car salesman.

I changed my clothes and got to work. I then find myself standing at the front door with about 20 other salesmen. I hear somebody shouting, I look over, and he's looking in my direction.

"Hey, green pea!"

I had never heard that term before, so I was sure he wasn't talking to me. I mean, no one was talking to me anyhow.

I later found out that he was talking to me. Even though he was shouting a name I didn't know the meaning, I thought it was great because I could tell that he was one of the best salesmen. He was just so cocky.

"What's a green pea??"

"You're a green pea. Just look at how green you are. You're a new salesman; a green pea."

Someone without any experience for what they are about to try. That's a green pea. He went on to tell me that the training manager wanted to see me.

Okay, now we're talking. I'm going to get trained.

I went to the office that was pointed out to me. When I walked in, I saw an older gentleman sitting behind a huge desk doing some kind of paperwork. He had a terrible rug on his head and reading glasses on the edge of his nose. He looked up at me over his glasses and did one of those silent, head-to-toe investigations of me.

In the meanest voice possible, this man barks, "What the f*** are you looking at?"

I went from feeling like a million bucks in my new three-piece polyester suit, to shaking in my shoes because of this guy.

"I was told that you were the training manager and since I am new here that you were going to train me."

"They told you what?"

"That you are the training manager and that you were going to train me."

He gave me that look over his glasses again and said, "Okay, follow me."

I follow him into this gigantic room filled with keys. Keys are all over the place. The wall was numbered from 0 to 9 across the top and 0 to 9 down the side. There were keys all over the desk. There were keys in folders on the floor. Keys were everywhere.

In a low gruff voice, he says, "Follow me."

He took me to the front of the store where the 20 salesmen are standing. By this time, all 20 of them and everyone else in the showroom is looking at me. He points outside and says, "There are the cars. Now sell something. And by the way, I'm not the goddamn training manager."

As you can imagine, everyone is laughing as hard as they can and having fun at my expense. I went over to the guy who set me up with the job and the suits, and I thanked him.

"What are you thanking me for?"

"For the lesson."

I thought to myself, *I'll never forget it and I'll never be that naïve again.*

I chalked it all up to being a green pea. All part of learning to be a car salesman. I have seen a lot of new guys come and go in this business and they are all treated the same way when they first start. Most people in the car business have a 90-day policy. There is no reason to get to know someone's name or to talk to the new guy in his first 90 days. That's because he probably won't be there in 90 days.

That was the mentality.

The new guys were so green; they would ask the dumbest questions. To give you an idea, a new guy started around Thanksgiving one year and asked a colleague if the dealership gave out turkeys for the holidays. The vet salesman answered without hesitation. "Yes, of course, we do. Doesn't everybody? Just go across the street to the grocery store. Go pick out the biggest, nicest turkey that they have. Take it up to the register, tell the cashier where you work and you won't be charged for the turkey." I don't remember anyone ever getting as mad as this poor green pea. When he got back, I could've sworn he was going to knock out the salesman who told him to go to the store.

And then, to not be outdone, a green pea once asked, "What do I do if I have three customers that want to test drive this regular-cab pickup truck? It only has a bench seat that holds three people. I know I have to go on every test drive. Where am I supposed to sit?" Again, someone spoke up right away without hesitation and said, "You're right. It's company policy. You have to go on all demo rides. Good news, we have a stool that you can place in the back of the pickup bed." This poor guy proceeded to ask every salesman where we kept the stool. Every salesman pointed to the next salesman and said, "He must have it, I don't have it." He couldn't keep the customer waiting much longer. Finally, this green pea just hopped in the bed of the pickup truck and served his duty. He went on the demo ride, suit and tie complete.

Chapter 4
First Day

With my initiation complete, or so I believed, and the laughter subsided, I am again at the front door with about 20 other salespeople.

"Why are we standing here?" I asked, hoping one of the 20 guys would answer.

"We're waiting for an 'up,'" someone blurted out.

I, of course, had no idea what an 'up' was.

I found it intriguing to watch the salesmen do nothing. Here I am, days after almost joining the Navy, eager to work, learn, and make some money. Some guys were talking about sports. Some were talking about where to get breakfast. Others were just staring out into space looking at the cars. I think the quiet ones staring off into space were new. Maybe not quite as new as I was.

Next thing we know, a car pulled into the parking lot. This car was old and in terrible shape. There was smoke coming out of the exhaust. As it got closer, you could see the dents in it. The rear bumper looked like it could fall off at any moment. I heard a salesman say, "What a POS."

Another salesman said, "They couldn't buy a car."

"Yeah, they probably have bad credit. That's why they are driving that POS."

And after the banter, the salesmen started to walk away. One after another until I found myself standing there by myself. I had no idea what was happening. *Where did everyone go?* One minute there were 20 guys standing there and the next, just me.

I was wondering how this would all play out. *What happens when a customer pulls in? Who gets to wait on them? Do all 20 salespeople rush toward the customer's car all at once and the fastest guy wins?* Well, this made it easy for me. I was the only guy there. I went out to say hello to the woman who got out of the car. Later on, I realize that the customer being a woman was one of the reasons everyone ran away. And of course, the car she pulled up in; which in some guy's minds led to bad credit, incapability of buying: no sale.

"Hi, how are you?" I asked.

She replied with a hello, seemingly nice enough. And then what I learnt later to be a typical response after approaching a customer, "I don't need any help."

"Well I'm new here and probably couldn't help much anyway. However, I do know where the keys are. So if you want to test drive something, I'm sure I can figure that out for you."

"I'm interested in a small pickup truck."

"Hey, that's great. My new friend who just hired me is actually the truck manager. Let me go ask him what trucks I should show you. I'm sure he'll give you a great deal."

He had me show her this yellow base model pickup that was in the back corner of the showroom. It had brown vinyl seats and a brown vinyl floor to match. It came with a four-speed manual transmission, no air conditioning, and no power steering. But it did have these great big chrome mirrors on the driver and passenger doors. I showed her the truck.

"This is exactly what I've been looking for!"

Really? I thought.

We went for a test ride, and she loved it even more. We went back inside, and my new friend helped me with the price. He then walked me through the paperwork process. I sold my first car. To my first customer too.

After she left and went *down the road busting bugs* as we say in the business, my friend came over to me. I was expecting a "Congratulations," or even just a "Good job." Nope. Nada. He said that the manager wanted to see me.

"That old guy with the glasses on his nose?"

"Yep, that's him."

"No way. I was in there once already today, and all he did was yell at me and try to embarrass me."

41

"Well, you have to see him. It'll be OK. You're just paying your dues."

Okay here goes. I stuck my head in the door to his office to see if it was safe to go inside. I slowly walked in to see the guy, and he gave me the same look over his glasses. After what seemed like an hour that he was staring at me, he called me by my last name, in a shouting but questioning form.

"BERMAN?!"

"Yes, that's right."

"Do you know what you did?"

"Yes I do. I did what you asked. I sold a car."

Maybe, here is where I'm told I did a great job. Maybe now is when I get congratulated. Nope.

In the same gruff voice, he barks, "Come here."

"Why?" I asked.

"Come here!"

So I walked ever so slowly towards him. I had no idea what was going on. I just sold my first car, and I was feeling pretty good about myself. Now here we have this very intimidating man yelling at me again. He's demanding I come closer to him. I'm standing in front of his desk, and he is standing directly behind the desk. We're at this stare down, and unbeknownst to me he opens his drawer and pulls out a pair of scissors. He grabbed my tie and yanked me towards him. I was shaking and yelling at him at the same time. Before I could finish what I was yelling, he cut my tie in half. Now I'm really mad. No more shaking. Just yelling.

"WHY DID YOU DO THAT? I DID WHAT YOU SAID. I SOLD A CAR. Well, a truck - IS THERE A DIFFERENCE?"

At this point, he's laughing at me. I assume everyone else was too.

"This isn't funny. I only have TWO TIES, and you just RUINED one of them!"

"You don't know what you just did. Let me explain it to you. That truck you just sold, it's the oldest vehicle that we have in inventory. It's had two birthdays here. No one could sell it for two years. You come in, and on your first day, you sold it. You didn't care that it was yellow. Or that it had vinyl seats. Or that it was a manual transmission. You didn't even know that someone ordered and put the wrong mirrors on the truck."

"Is that why you cut my tie?"

"No, I cut your tie because that's tradition. When you sell your first car, you get your tie cut. You have to wear it like that all day. It's a conversation piece. It should help you to sell another vehicle. And by the way, that two-year-old truck that you sold has a $500 spiff on it."

And with that, he handed me five crisp Benjamins. He shook my hand, and I got my first "Good job," followed by, "Welcome to the car business."

$500 back then was like a couple thousand dollars now. What a great feeling that was. As soon as I left his office, I headed right over to my new friend and paid him back for the suit. Then I took him to lunch. AND I paid. I got hooked on the car business on my first day.

Chapter 5
Managers

From the outside looking in, it looks like the job to have. One of the problems is that most managers have no idea how to manage people. First, you have to ask, how did they get that job? How did they become the manager of a multimillion dollar operation? They couldn't even manage themselves, let alone a sales team.

So how do they get that job? They probably sold a couple of cars; maybe they have a little bit of experience in the business. That and the recent sales manager got fired because the numbers weren't where the owners wanted them to be. Not that the numbers were based on anything. The manufacturer gives the dealer a target number to hit each month, but then the owner would just double or triple it and hand the new made-up number to the manager. Keep in mind that the manufacturer pays people to research these numbers. Market researchers, data analyzers, number crunchers. These experts analyze more data than we can imagine. The dealer isn't researching data; his toys and vacations keep him busy enough.

The new manager is doomed even before he starts. Like in a sales role, there isn't any training. Have you ever heard of a sales manager school? So the new manager only knows how to do the job based on the way the previous manager did it, and he just got fired for doing it that way.

Most sales managers in the car business are lazy. Take for example the practice of sending a salesperson back-and-forth with a customer. Everyone loves that. I never understood why. You've probably seen this or have been the customer sitting at the desk. Your salesman is sitting with you; you ask a question, he leaves to go ask his manager. The salesman comes back, and the same scenario happens again, and maybe again. I've heard some say that if the sales manager comes to actually speak to the customer that he will have to give them a price. Maybe even a lower price. Well, they can't buy the car without a price. So what are these managers afraid of? They have no problem giving a lower price to the salesman to take to the customer, but they won't get up to talk to the customer themselves. And you know the customer only wants to negotiate with the sales manager anyway. No wonder, so many sales managers get fired. As soon as they get the title, they mysteriously forget where they came from.

They seem to instantly forget that they were once (and truly still are) a salesman. They have forgotten that they used to complain about how lazy the managers were. That they wouldn't help or care to help the salesmen.

It looks and seems like a glamorous position. Usually, they are the best dressed, and they have the privilege of sitting up high in the tower not having to beat the bricks, as we say. They don't have to wait on customers or walk the lot showing cars anymore. The managers get paid on the salesmen's commissions. Glorious right? Not so fast. With that position also comes even more hours. Now you have to be the first one in and the last one out. Now you get keys to the multimillion-dollar operation. And you have to love the calls in the middle of the night. Because guess what? The sales manager is now on the security list. That alarm goes off a lot. Who knows why? Very little is ever stolen from inside a car dealership. Outside the dealership is another story. It could be the mice; it could be from the balloons that were put out earlier that day. Anything could set off the motion sensors.

I was offered my first sales manager job six months into the business. I was still a green pea as far as I was concerned. I didn't really know the business. I didn't understand why so many people were coming and going. Quitting or getting fired. I was happy selling cars. I was making three times as much as I was when I was spinning pizzas. I went from making $12,000 a year to $36,000 a year. I had money, and I had money in the bank. All was well.

Then they wanted me to be a manager. Come to find out; they needed someone to watch the desk when they left. Or when they went down to the basement to do whatever it is you do in the basement of a dealership. I didn't even know that there was a basement. Why would I? I never had to go down there. There weren't any cars or customers down there. So when they wanted to go down there and hide they would page me as the mushroom.

You could hear it over the loudspeaker.

"Mushroom to the sales desk. Mushroom to the sales desk."

Then you get your first check. Your first manager's pay. You are expecting this huge raise. Extra zeros maybe. But it's nowhere near what you expected it to be. You've done the math over and over again. You know what the check should have been. It should've been for a certain amount. However, it was for much less. Yes, you did the math, but the dealer has a comptroller, and an accountant that is much better at the math than any of us will ever be.

It was never where it was supposed to be. If you asked for an explanation, you were told about the fictitious charges to the bottom line that we were getting paid. After a while, you would put up with it if it was enough money. Or you simply allowed for a percentage of the difference from what you thought your pay should be for the month. I figured that if it was within 5% of what I thought it should be, I wouldn't argue. It wasn't worth the aggravation. When it became not worth the aggravation and the money, I went back on the floor. Most times I made more money selling cars than as a manager. Some managers had a problem with this. They couldn't handle a guy below them making more money. Their ego just wouldn't let them. When I held a management role, I can tell you I never had a problem with it. If a salesman made more money than the manager, he earned it.

So you think you want to be a sales manager? Try the "Ben Franklin close" on yourself. It's also called, "The balance sheet close." List the pros and cons. Draw a line down the middle of your paper. On the left-hand side write the word 'pros,' and on the right-hand side write the word 'cons.'

Pros	Cons

OK, so what are the pros to being a sales manager? For one, it's a prestigious position; you get paid on what the other salesmen sell, and you're off the showroom floor. The title boosts the ego.

Pros	Cons
• Prestige	
• Ego	

Now for the cons: longer hours, never knowing what you're going to get paid, can get fired at any moment, no training, more responsibility, have to handle all the complaints. There are many more cons.

Pros	Cons
• Prestige	• Longer hours
• Ego	• Unknown pay
	• Lack of job security
	• No training
	• More responsibility

Both ways it's a thankless position, and you're always on the bubble. You will always have to take the blame if something goes wrong. Just imagine if you don't have enough cars out. It won't be the salesmen's fault. They are actually harder to replace than you are. You on the other hand, as a manager, are easy to replace. There are at least 10 to 15 guys on the floor right now hoping for what they think would be a promotion. They're willing to endure the cons of being a sales manager, even though most of them don't yet know what those might be. For some reason, some of the guys pounding the bricks want to trade their job security and life of ease for a prestigious title.

Chapter 6
Meetings

Why? Why do we have so many meetings? And why do we have so many meetings about nothing?

I think long ago, someone from the corporate world came over to the car business. They wanted to make the car business more like what they were used to. So they implemented meetings. A lot of meetings. The problem is that they didn't teach anyone how to conduct a meeting. Just like they promoted someone to manage the place. They didn't train him either. They just assumed he could do the job.

I don't think it's right for everyone to have to go to a meeting when the person holding the meeting didn't prepare for it. We call that winging it.

You already learned about the Saturday morning meeting. But there's also the Monday morning meeting. Like the Saturday meeting, Monday's usually started before 9 AM - let's say 8:30 AM. The dreaded Monday morning meeting has become known as the Monday morning *beating*. We now have the Saturday morning meeting and the Monday morning beating. It didn't matter how well you did leading up to it; they would always find something wrong. The beating was held on Monday because all of the salesmen were there on Monday mornings. Monday was the second biggest day of the week. No one was scheduled off on Saturday or Monday.

What could be wrong with selling and delivering 20 cars on a Saturday? What could they possibly be mad at? How ever many cars we sold, their goal was always higher. We could sell 20 cars, and they would say that their goal was 25 or 30. Even though on Saturday morning they preached 20 as our target. It was never enough. And your grosses sucked.

"You're giving them away!"

"You're not doing your job. It's obvious by the gross."

"I don't know what you're selling out there, but it's not cars. And what is with all the cash deals? Why are you not selling our financing to your customers?"

This will go on for about an hour. So now it's 9:30 and you have to pick yourself up after listening to all of this for an hour. No one else was going to motivate you.

Okay, that's the first meeting of the day. Then a manager is supposed to come over and sit down with you and go over your unsold customers. He is supposed to help you with whatever you're struggling with.

What really happens in this one-on-one meeting between you and the manager is comical. You would think this meeting is a good thing. Well on paper it does look good. One-on-one time with your boss. I mean he was a great salesman, right? That's how he got the position right? He's going to spend some time with you and show you how to be a great salesman like he was right? Nope. Again, not so fast. He has no intentions of spending time with you.

He sits down and says, "OK, we are going to do our daily one-on-one meeting. Do you have anything working today?"

Here's what should be happening: you and your manager go through your customers that you have logged into your CRM, and he should call some of them for you. He should use this as a teaching moment. But he doesn't want to sit there with you. He wants to go sit up on the tower. So he says, "Call your customers back. Make some appointments. I'll be over there if you need me."

The next morning there is another meeting at 9 AM at the tower or sales desk. Same questions are asked.

Each salesperson present is asked, "How many appointments do *you* have? None? How are you going to make a living? I'm wondering the same thing."

Really all they are asking is for the salesmen to lie to them. Because if you don't have any appointments, you can't wait on anybody until you do. You just tell them you have an appointment or two. It's not like they're going to call and confirm your appointments. That would be the right thing to do. That would be like real work. Let's be honest. The 9 AM meeting every morning is just rollcall.

So you have a couple of meetings every day until something else comes up. They can page for all salesmen to come to the sales desk multiple times a day. That's how communication is done at the car dealership. Through beatings at the sales desk after being paged over the intercom. The managers seem to love the paging system.

Now to be fair, some of the managers began to get it. Some of the better managers would prepare for the meetings. They would have an agenda and make it a positive meeting.

I worked for a manager who loved his Saturday morning meetings. He would come up with some of the greatest motivational tools ever. One Saturday morning, in particular, we are seated around this huge conference table, and there is a big brown paper grocery bag in the center of the table. He started off the meeting pumping us up about Saturday. How great today is going to be. How we have this ad out. Best ad yet. We are going to sell a ton of cars off of it. Even had a copy of the ad. That's a good manager. He even explained it to us. He made it a positive ad. We'll talk about advertising later. Back to the meeting.

All the while, we were all wondering what's in the bag. He finished explaining the ad and then asked the group, "Any questions?"

Almost in unison, we reply, "What's in the bag??"

This was not normal. The bag was really out of place.

"You want to see what's in the bag?"

Yes, we do. He left the head of the table, grabbed the bag, and went back to the head of the table. He then turned the bag sideways and threw the contents of the bag toward all of us. Then all of a sudden, there are people jumping on the table. Pushing each other out of the way. He had money in the bag. Lots of cash money. The money was everywhere. People are going crazy grabbing as much as they could. Now that's what I call motivational. Giving out money before the day started.

In another meeting with the same manager a couple weeks later, there was no bag on the table.

"Why isn't there a bag of money? We sold you 30 cars Saturday."

I think the actual number was 28.

He said, "You want more money? If I give you more money will that guarantee me 25 sales today?"

Emphatically we all agreed that yes it would.

"OK, look under your chairs."

And with that, we all jumped up and turned our chairs upside down. Taped underneath each of our chairs was a different amount of cash. It was the luck of the draw as to where you sat. And it was the luck of the draw as to how much was under your chair. I was just wondering what time this guy got there to put the money under each chair.

This particular manager could motivate the sales team. He knew how to talk to us. He came from the sales floor and he never ever forgot where he came from. That's a great manager.

Chapter 7
The Old Days

Ah, the old days. Life was much simpler back then. Life as a car salesman was simpler, yet harder at the same time.

In the old days, we didn't have computers. Everything was done by hand. We were our own computers. We had to keep track of our customers on our own.

I was told once that if you kept your name in front of your customers four times a year, that as a sales person you would have enough repeat and referral business that you wouldn't have to stand at the front door to wait and fight all the other salespeople for an 'up.'

I figured out early on that I needed a system. So I bought a box with 3 x 5 index cards and filed them by month. I used that as my birthday file. Every time I got somebody's name and address, I would make sure I got their birthday as well. If they had their license that made it easy. As I started to sell cars, I made a folder to keep track of all my monthly sales. All my sold deals. I also had a 3-ring binder on my desk with a daily action plan. At the beginning of the month, I had to go through it and date each and every page from the first day of the month 'til the last day of the month. Well, without Excel, you had to do it by hand. And since this business is based on monthly performance, I had each month set up and ready to go.

My birthday file was growing. Everyone that caught wind of my scheme wanted a birthday card. Even the ladies in the accounting office. They saw me stamping my birthday cards at the stamp machine. They would ask why they didn't get a birthday card. I said, "I'll be right back." I went to my desk and grabbed a 3 x 5 file card and went right back into the accounting office. I said "It's because I don't have a file card for your birthday. I'll fill one out right now, and you'll get a birthday card from me from now on."

That was the first thing I did every morning when I got to work. I grabbed a cup of coffee, went four days ahead in my file box. Hand wrote all my birthday cards. Then I went to my thank-you notes; to whomever I waited on the day before and then the thank-you notes to those I sold to the day before. Utilizing my monthly sales folders, I also sent anniversary cards to the people who bought a car from me. I was mailing out 20 to 25 pieces of mail a day. It just became a habit, an easy one at that.

If I had your birthday and address, I sent you a birthday card. Even if you bought elsewhere. One time a customer called me after he received a birthday card from me. He told me that I could stop sending him cards because he bought another brand, from another store.

"Would it be okay if I continued to send cards to be able to stay in touch?" I asked. I also assured this customer that it was okay that he bought something else. I let him in on the secret that I can't sell everyone a car. I would just like the opportunity to do so.

"However, if you like the service I gave you, and you know somebody in the market for the brand that I sell (that was Toyota at the time) would you refer them to me?"

"Of course," he replied. "You were great. I just liked the Honda better."

I understood, and I thanked him.

And so it went. I had two or three 3 x 5 file boxes on my desk after just a couple of years of doing this. I had a great amount of repeat and referral customers coming to the dealership and asking for me. One customer in particular I remember was a young woman. I was with a customer at the time at my desk when she walked into the showroom and was greeted by another salesperson. With my desk being upfront near the door I heard her say, "I'm looking for the salesman that sold my roommate a car. He sent her a birthday card. I don't know his name but could you look him up for me by my roommate's name?"

The salesman lowered his head and said, "I don't have to look it up. The salesman you're looking for is Rick. He's right over there. He's the only one who sends out birthday cards."

She waited for me to finish up with my current customer. Within a few hours, she had purchased a car from me.

Everyone I worked with (in addition to my customers and their friends) knew that I sent out birthday cards. Everyone knew that the gesture of sending cards sold cars for me. But no one else wanted to put the extra time in to do it.

Selling cars in the old days took longer because everything was done by hand. I know it doesn't seem like computers have streamlined the process because it still takes three hours to buy a car. Not only was the paperwork different, but so were the managers. They were actually better. They had to be. However, this was before the human resources department was even a concept. We had a finance manager for example, at the time who controlled the dealership. He was allowed to say or do anything he wanted because he made the dealership a lot of money. More money than any of the other departments. He was what you would call, 'strong in the box.' And if he didn't like you or you didn't do what he wanted you to do, your deal went to the back of the line. He didn't care about your customer, nor did he care if they were next or last for finance. We figured out this guy's motives, and I narrowed them down to two: 1) making money. Was it a finance deal? Because if the customer was paying cash or had their own loan through their own bank, it didn't matter how much he liked you. That deal was going to be last. He was going to do the finance deals that he can make money on first.

The second way to get your deal into his queue was by way of a little bribery. Imagine the time before the Internet. Before computers and before cell phones. This was a time when CDs (compact discs) were replacing cassette tapes. They were the hottest thing on the market. So if you had a deal and you wanted your people to get into the finance office, you had better have the latest CD that was out. Because he wanted it. He wanted you to pay for it, and he wanted you to give it to him. This guy never paid for lunch or dinner either. He actually controlled your destiny. There wasn't CSI (customer satisfaction index) back then either. It really didn't matter how the customer or the salespeople were spoken to or treated.

Being a salesman back then was the job to have. For the most part, salesmen really were their own boss. Salesmen had a couple of rules to follow, but they were basically on their own. As a salesman, if I wanted to get lost I could. It's not like they could text me. Or "find my iPhone." The way I looked at it was the dealer supplied me with the desk, the product to sell, and he advertised for me. The rest was up to me. It was my business. I could set it up anyway that I wanted. I would go as far as to pick my customers car up for service in the morning to save them time and the inconvenience of coming into the service department.

Speaking of service, we had a great service department back then. I really feel like they were way ahead of their time. They had a team concept. When a car came in it was placed on a team. Blue team, green team, red, or silver team. That way the same team always worked on your car. They got to know you and your car. So I had color coordinated key rings made up that matched the team that the car was on. The key rings had my name, the dealership name, address, and phone number. Again, I was the only one who did that.

My name was in front of my customers every day. It was my business. I had to promote myself. Other than the meetings and beatings, selling cars back then was really fun. The technology was changing rapidly. We were selling a lot of cars at the time. You had a choice back then to make. Are you going to change with the times? Or are you going to be the dinosaur, refusing to accept everything new that was coming?

Chapter 8
The 21st Century

What does the life of a car salesman look like now? I can tell you we still come in early for the Monday morning meeting. For the most part, the managers have evolved. They don't yell as much. The Monday morning beatings have turned into Monday morning meetings. We discuss the weekend. What went well and what could have been better. We get a 'state of the union' on where we are. In other words, we're updated on how many cars the dealership has out, and how much gross we have made on them thus far.

Since the reinstatement of the human resources department, the name-calling and the cursing has really been cut down to a minimum.

The first task of the day hasn't changed between then and now. It remains coffee, first. Next, take it to your first meeting of the day. Nowadays though, when the meeting is over you go to your desk and turn on your computer. What a difference the wonderful technology has made. Once the computer boots up, your daily work plan is right there in front of you. Nice, neat and in order. All the phone calls that you have to make that day are listed there on the screen. The better the notes that you keep on the computer, the easier the calls will be. A good salesman will make between 25 and 50 calls a day. I also know of salespeople, the exceptional ones, who make 100 calls a day.

You have to get your day in order. Organizational skills are a must now. You really can't get by without them. You see the phone calls that have to be made, now think about the mailings that have to be sent out. Some of it can be emailed. However, the thank you cards, and birthday cards, should still be handwritten. Old school, snail-mail.

Back in the 80's, as mentioned earlier, I was sending out 20 to 25 handwritten letters a day. Nowadays, a good salesperson should be doing double that.

There is always something to do. In between phone calls and mail-outs, salesmen should still have a day planned with appointments, and getting cars ready for test drives and any deliveries that you may have set up. I believe that activity breeds activity. Therefore, I always came to work *to* work. You wouldn't find me in the group of guys on the showroom floor. I was not interested in what was for breakfast or lunch. I ate my breakfast before I came in so that when I got there, I was ready to hit the floor running. I always went out to lunch though. I took a little break from the dealership to do some outside prospecting. I would walk around the mall and hand out my business cards. I made sure everyone knew what I did for a living.

The five 12-hour days per week are now reduced to three 12-hour days per week. Most dealerships will also give their salesmen a morning off. Mornings tend to be less busy than evenings; which makes sense since most people work until five or 6 PM. If you're lucky though, you get a night off along with your morning off. Honestly, after working five 12-hour shifts a week for so long, three 12-hour shifts seemed really easy. Then to get a night off and a morning off? I might not know what to do with all the free time.

After lunch, if you didn't have an appointment, the rest of the afternoon is used to set up tomorrow. If you get through that, you set up your days going forward and then you set up your weekend. You want to make sure that you have as many appointments as you possibly can. Also, somewhere in between your phone calls is your daily one on one meeting with your manager. That could take anywhere from 20 minutes to an hour. It was up to you on how much time you wanted, or needed to spend with him.

There are also certifications to complete. Salesmen have a slew of online classes to take to be certified in the brand that they're selling. The certification modules were very time-consuming. Some certification courses were better than others. If it was real world stuff, I liked it. I couldn't get enough of good factory training. Who knows the vehicles better than they do? There was always one guy in the dealership who knew the cars and the information inside and out. We all knew the basic stuff, but he knew the off-the-wall stuff too. When someone wanted to know what year they stopped making a certain model, he knew that. He knew all the crazy color names as well. For example, remember the lime green Mustangs? Do you know what the color name was? It was called *Gotta Have It Green*. I'm not making this up. Someone really got paid for coming up with that name.

So this particular guy was considered our product specialist. For some reason, he never really sold a lot of cars, but he knew all about them. It would've been great if he had done the delivery on the car as well.

This is an area that I excelled in. I was so happy for the customer. I knew that this is the second largest purchase a person makes in their lifetime. Their home is the largest. I wanted my customers to have an excellent experience from the moment they walked in, until the time they left in their new car. I even ensured that the positive experience continued; whether it was when they were back for service, if they needed anything in between, or when they were ready for their next car. I made sure that they got a delivery that no one else was taking the time to do. I made sure they knew where everything was on their new car before they left. This could take over an hour on some of the models. I would start by walking around the car with a customer. I have already inspected the car way before the customer saw it.

I made sure it was cleaned properly and didn't have any marks on it or any issues. I always took care of the lot guys who clean the cars for deliveries. They have one of the most important jobs in the dealership. They also have the most thankless job. These guys are really underappreciated for how hard they work. In the hot summer months, I always bought them Gatorade and water. The wash bay area would usually be outside in the heat. It's also wet, and a lot of these guys couldn't afford waterproof shoes. I'd always see them in their tennis shoes. Those things would be ruined first thing in the morning on the first car that was cleaned. They would wear wet shoes all day long. I can't tell you how many pairs of waterproof shoes I bought for some of these guys who could not afford them.

Okay, back to delivering the car. When the walk around was done, I had the new owner sit in the driver seat. I started on the driver's door. Making sure they knew how everything on the door worked. Most times that's where the mirrors are. So we set the mirrors first. Showed them how the windows worked. Then moved to the driver seat. I showed them all the different adjustments for the seat and then went ahead and set the seat for them to their most comfortable driving position. Then, we would save everything into the memory on the driver's door. Next, was the left side of the dash. Lights, maybe even the cruise control. Onto the wipers, then the controls on the steering wheel. Now I moved into the passenger seat and went over the heat and air-conditioning systems. Then came the radio, navigation, and of course, the Bluetooth. I set everyone's phone and made them call me so that they would have my number in their cell phone. If they had any questions or concerns, I wanted to be the first one that they called. I invited them to come back anytime if they didn't know where something was or how something worked with the new car before driving in traffic. I did not want them to be looking for the lights or the windshield wipers while they were driving. I even offered to go for another test ride if they wanted.

Such is the life of a car salesman today. It's still a lot of hours. Not as many as before. It is still as mentally difficult as ever. But as far as I'm concerned, it's still fun. It's still so thrilling, and truly rewarding, to help someone buy (or lease) a new car. To see the smile on someone's face as they are taking delivery of their brand new automobile is an incredibly awesome feeling.

Chapter 9
Advertising

Ever wonder where the bad rap on car salesmen comes from? I've been in the business for over 30 years, and I can honestly say that I do not deserve that bad reputation. That being said, I can tell you where it stems from.

When I first got into the car business, I was so naïve that I didn't even know how lowly the profession was considered.

I remember when I told my mother. Mind you, this was days after I was supposed to be shipped off to boot camp.

"Mom, I got a new job. I'm going to be a car salesman."

"Oh no," she cried. "Not that. Please, anything except a car salesman."

"Why, Mom?"

"Car salesmen have a terrible reputation!"

"Well, I don't know anything about that. But if that's the case, I'll change our reputation one customer at a time."

That's exactly what I did, and what I continue to do.

Maybe I've kept my reputation intact because I never wore a plaid sport coat with plaid slacks that didn't match. I believe that the clothes some of the guys wore in the old days didn't do anything to help the reputation. Have you ever heard the expression, *'He looks like a used car salesman?'* I have sold used cars, and I've even been a used car manager before.

Thankfully though, I've never been accused of 'looking' the part.

So, the typical wardrobe was one reason for the bad reputation. Another reason was due to the advertising. The car business did not invent advertising. I think the industry just adopted it and then stretched it to its limits. Now, it seems that a lot of the ads that are being used by other businesses mimic the car ads.

How many times have you seen an ad that says, *'As low as...?'* That one didn't get us into much trouble, did it? We call that ad a *price leader*. A price leader is when a dealer advertises a particular vehicle for the lowest price possible. He would take everything that he possibly could out of the price so that he could advertise it that way. Oh, don't worry, they would add it all back in later! And then some. So many things are wrong with this three-word-ad.

The first thing that you have to do is read the fine print. The fine print - which is always too small to read - is always filled with attorney b.s. That fine print is now read out loud at a rapid pace by the commercial narrator. That way, the consumer is unable to understand the stipulations. For example:

OUR MOST LUXURIOUS VEHICLE, as low as $12,999!

Plus taxes and tags. Plus freight. Options and dealer installed equipment extra. Price subject to change. At least $4,000 due at signing. Subject to availability. See your local dealer for more details.

The dealers thought it was a good idea to advertise the car for a price they didn't want to sell it for. They would bring you in on that low price and then tell you that the car was sold. The ONE car they were showing on the ad. They would proceed to try to sell you a more expensive car, or anything else that they had on the lot. That tactic is known as *bait and switch*. Thus, the fine print, now that *bait and switch* is illegal. The fine print, in the dealer's eyes, justifies the bait. The bait and switch tactic is still one of the reasons for the industry's terrible reputation.

Once the salesman has the customer in front of him, he usually goes on to boast about how great he is. How he will take care of you. And, after all of that, it still takes him over three hours to complete the paperwork.

If you have to explain the fine print, and you know going in that the ad is misleading, and that it is certainly going to upset customers, why advertise that way? Why would you want to upset your customers? You only have one vehicle at that price, right? So, then how many customers will you chase away that will never come back and do business with you? And we should be willing to lose all of those potential customers for ONE sale? It's a sale that you don't even want to make. At the low price that it is advertised, there really isn't any profit in that deal. There's always hope to make a profit on the other transactions associated, such as the products and warranties sold in finance. There's also hope that there's a trade-in to go with that deal. There's hope that the difference that was lost in selling the car at such a low price can be made up with the trade-in.

I can tell you that the ads have gotten worse over the years. At first, the ads were simple. They didn't even display a price. The ads were solely about the car and its features. The first ads that featured pricing in the early days were presented in a day before negotiating. The price was the price. Really, how much car could they negotiate when the car was listed for $1,000? Soon after, the price inflated to $2,000. There still wasn't any negotiating.

The automotive industry didn't delve into the *discount age* until much later. Someone studied supply and demand and adjusted accordingly. There wasn't need to discount when there was the right amount of cars for the right amount of public demand.

Things started to change around World War II. All of the manufacturing plants were converted into military factories. These huge facilities went from building automobiles to building tanks, airplanes, and ammunition. Cars were not in production for a few years. Supply started to dwindle.

Due to the low supply and continued demand, some of the dealers began charging far more than what the cars were worth. Forget about a discount. This was the industry's first black eye. Remember we're talking about used cars being sold at a higher price since there weren't any new cars being built. The used cars became very expensive because there were very few available to the public. The dealers took advantage of this and charged as much as they could for the vehicles that were available at the time.

As the war neared its end, soldiers were returning home. They had money in their pockets, and they needed transportation. However, cars hadn't been built in a few years. There were only used cars for sale, expensive ones at that. Plants began building new cars, and they were re-emerging into the market. This evolution is what ignited the expression, *'Forget about the sticker.'*

The sticker displays the price of the car.

"This is what you're going to pay for it, Mr. Customer."

Take a look at the lot, do you see any other cars?

Another black eye.

From that point on, new cars were sold for more than the sticker price. For the first time, the dealer began charging too much for new cars. This particular tactic was learned when selling used cars in short supply.

This went on for a while. At least until supply caught up with demand. The demand stayed about the same, but the factories got back to producing at full capacity. Cars were being shipped to the dealers as quickly as they were being produced. All of a sudden, the dealerships had cars on their lots. For the first time, the supply exceeded the demand. The dealer had never been in that situation.

Now, they needed to get rid of the cars that were essentially costing money just sitting there. Being the brilliant owner that he is, he took out an ad in the local paper. The ad offered an absurd discount. This is another first - the dealer having to discount cars.

This worked for a while. The post-war automotive era brought us into the *discount era* of advertising. I'm not sure if Sears and Roebuck started this form of advertising or if a car dealer did. But one of them saw an ad in the paper and thought: *Hey that's a great idea. We should do that.*

That was around the time that all the dealers got into discounting their cars. They all went from giving their customers the highest prices to competing to offer the lowest prices. That's also around the time we forgot about the customer. The customer no longer mattered. Each dealer's edge (and ego) was what mattered. Which dealer could come up with the best ad to undercut their competition? Who was the cleverest advertiser? Even those in the business watched the ads get slimier and slimier. We slime-less guys just hoped that we didn't work for a dealer that played in that arena.

This new selling tactic surely wasn't fun for a salesman. To have to wait on a customer, and then to have them ask for the car that was advertised in the paper. You were the lucky one to have to relay the lie:

"Good news, that one is sold, but I have one almost just like it right over here, follow me."

In summation, the bad reputation of our industry has definitely been earned. Not by all, and not by most of the generation of salespeople selling cars nowadays. However, the current generation still hasn't done as much as they possibly can to change that. There is so much more to do. Even so, don't give up on your local car salesperson. It's probably not their fault.

Chapter 10
The Good, the Bad, and the Ugly

As you have gathered from the previous nine chapters, there's a lot of good, bad, and ugly in the automobile business. Let's revisit the *bad*.

If you didn't know before, now you know that car salespeople have a bad reputation. There isn't much fun in having to justify what you do for a living. *Bad*. It didn't take long for me to realize just how many people look down on you once they find out that you sell cars. *Bad*.

I was told early on in my career to make sure that everyone I came into contact with knew what I did for a living. I cannot tell you how many people made faces at me before asking with disgust, "You sell cars?" It was always asked in such a derogatory way that I felt the need to defend myself. *Bad*.

"Yes, I do. Why do you ask that way? Is there something wrong with that?"

You would have thought that I was a bank robber or something.

"Oh no… it's just that… well you know, no one likes a car salesman."

"Why not?" I would ask. "What have I done to you? Or anyone else for that matter?"

Bad.

That is why, from day one, I have tried so hard to change that. I will never give up on teaching and coaching how to take care of the customer to stop the stereotype.

As a group of people, as an industry, we must become more professional. We are selling a big-tickct item. It is *had* to see a new salesperson start and not receive any training. The manufacturers are making an effort to change this by way of offering and requiring online product training and certification. However, there is so much more that goes into the sale of a vehicle. The first priority should be the customer and his or her needs. This falls on the dealer. If sales training was made available, the professionalism would improve dramatically.

Now for the *ugly*. There is also a lot of this going on in our business. Let's start with the time missed with your family. Time is something that you can never get back. If you've ever had to make a decision between going to your kid's birthday party and working, you are likely in the car business.

Ugly.

Have you ever given up going to the mall, or a movie, or even going out to dinner with your spouse because you thought you had a delivery at the dealership? *Ugly.* You can never get this time back either. The divorce rate in this country is around 50%. I would bet that the divorce rate in the car business is much higher than that.

Ugly.

Having to fight for your pay, is *ugly*. Nothing good can come from that. Commission-based pay plans encompass a huge grey area. *Based* being the optional word in that sentence. You never really know what your pay is based on. There are always parameters. There are parameters for you, and parameters for them.

The last *ugly* item I'll touch on is this thing called '*Employment at will.*' If you have never heard of it, it is when you can quit anytime without notice, and the employer can fire you anytime without notice. Most times without reason.

I have seen guys come back from an earned (and approved) vacation to find their belongings in a box on the floor. *Ugly*. His replacement is sitting in what was his seat at his desk. That's really *ugly*. He comes back to receive the news of his firing, from his replacement!

Ugly.

It certainly is a tough business. Tougher than it has to be. To make up for all the bad and all the ugly in our business is the compensation. If you have a little bit of talent, you can make a nice living. An above average income at that. If you have even more talent and are willing to learn the business, the sky's the limit. If you can learn to listen to the successful people in and out of the automobile business, you can truly make as much money as you want.

You have to be honest, caring, and compassionate. You have to find a product that you love and believe in. You have to stay with the product. Hopefully, you can find a dealer with those same qualities so that you can stay with them for years to come.

Then it becomes fun. Selling cars won't feel like a job anymore. You made a name for yourself. People know where you are. They come to see you. They ask for you by name. You've made your customers happy, and they're telling everyone about you.

Now you're winning contests. You're winning trips. I won trips to San Francisco, Orlando, Vegas, and even Hawaii. I even won a brand new car. I sold it back to the dealer and put that money down on a brand new house.

There is more good in the car business than there is ugly. It really is just what you make of it. I made it mine. It was *my* desk and *my* customers in front of me. The dealer advertised and supplied the product for me. I always felt that I was in business for myself. This is how I have always treated my customers. The same way that I would want to be treated. I am a customer as well. It is the same way I represented the dealership. I represented it as if my name was on the building. When a situation came up, before acting or making a decision,

I would always ask myself, "*How would the dealer [whose name is on the building] handle this?*"

Henry Ford once said, "It is not the employer who pays your wages. It is the customer. The employer only administers it."

When the Model-T first came out in mass production, Mr. Ford said that his customers could get it in any color they wanted. As long as it was black.

The Glossary

Car Lingo

1. **Addendum** - Something added. An additional sticker added to the MSRP. Also known as the Bump sticker.

2. **Back End** - The profit made on a deal in the finance office.

3. **The Box** - The office in which the final paperwork is completed on a deal.

4. **Broom** - Used for sweeping things away. In this case, brooming a customer.

5. **Car Lawyer** - Someone who negotiates the price of a car for someone other than themselves.

6. **Cash Deal** - A deal where the customer opts out of the financing offered by the dealer. The customer brings in the amount owed for the car by arranging their own loan with their bank or credit union. The customer can also actually write a check.

7. **CRM** - Customer Relationship Management. A computer software program that organizes all information pertinent to selling a car.

8. **CSI** - Customer Satisfaction Index. The culmination of scores as surveyed by the customers who have purchased a car.

9. **De-horse** - To take a customer out of their car and put them in another one. For example, an extended test drive.

10. **The Desk** - The place where the sales managers sit and work the deals the salespeople bring to them.

11. **F&I** - Stands for Finance and Insurance, also known as the business office of the dealership. This is where the customer goes to pay for the automobile that they just purchased. They are offered various ways to finance their vehicle and purchase additional products.

12. **(The) Floor** - The showroom floor.

13. **Floor Plan** - The vehicles sitting on the dealer's lots are financed by the bank, and then interest is paid on that loan on a monthly basis.

14. **Front End** - The gross profit made from the actual sale of the automobile.

15. **Green Pea** - Being brand new at something. Being green. A new salesperson. Not having any experience.

16. **Grinder** - A customer who continues to negotiate for a long period of time. He or she grinds out a deal.

17. **Gross** - The profit on a deal.

18. **Hand Shaker** - Another term for a manual shift vehicle.

19. **Home Run** - When an above average gross profit is made on a deal. Usually, if a customer pays MSRP or higher.

20. **Lay-Down** - A customer who does not ask any questions about the price and agrees to all of the dealer's terms.

21. **Left Side** - The left side of the book used to appraise the vehicle. The left side is higher than the right side. The left side refers to extra clean or clean value.

22. **Low-Ball** - The act of giving a lower price than you're willing to sell the vehicle for. For example, to low-ball, a customer is to give them a price that no one else can match so that the customer has to come back to your store for the last shot at selling them a car.

23. **Mini (A mini-deal)** - A lower than average gross profit deal. In return, a minimum commission paid to the salesperson.

24. **Monroney Sticker** - The Monroney sticker, also known as the window sticker, is a label that is federally required to be displayed on all new vehicles. It includes certain information about that vehicle such as equipment, options, and price. It was named after Oklahoma Senator Almer Stilwell "Mike" Monroney in 1958.

25. **MSRP** - Manufacturer's Suggested Retail Price.

26. **Mushroom** - A term used to describe a person who is kept in the dark, and fed a bunch of crap.

27. **Pack** - An amount of money that the dealer takes from a deal before any gross profit is calculated to cover said expenses.

28. **Pencil** - The offer written on a worksheet by a manager to be presented to a customer by a salesperson. This is

usually done in a certain color sharpie. The color depends on the manager's preference.

29. **P.O.S.** - A vehicle that is in really bad condition. It is actually an acronym for Piece of Shit.

30. **Right Side** - The right-hand side of the wholesale book used to appraise the vehicle. The right side refers to the rough book, as defined under "Rough Book."

31. **Rat** - A customer who is credit-challenged and is unable to finance a car.

32. **Rough Book** - A term used to appraise the vehicle, which refers to the under-average or rough condition value.

33. **Skating** - Taking another salesperson's customer, or deal. Imagine someone having roller skates on to skate around or to be faster than the other salespeople.

34. **Spiff** - A special reward, extra commission or amount of money that is paid to a salesperson that is not in the written payment plan.

35. **Split Deal** - When two salespeople are involved in a sale of a vehicle, and they split the commission.

36. **Spot** - Refers to a spot delivery. When a customer buys a vehicle on the spot, as opposed to leaving and returning at a later date to take delivery of the vehicle.

37. **Squirrel** - A customer that does not know what they want to buy. A customer that spends time with the salesperson and a sale cannot be reached.

38. **Stroker** - A customer that asked for a price and then negotiates a price without a commitment and without purchasing the vehicle.

39. **T. D.** - A deal that is turned down. As in turned down for financing from the bank.

40. **Three on a Tree** - A manual transmission vehicle where the shifter is mounted on the steering column.

41. **T. O.** - Stands for turnover. When a salesperson has not closed the customer and then has to turn the customer over to a manager so that he or she can try and close that customer.

42. **Tower** - Another term for the desk where the deals are worked. The tower is usually higher than the other desks so that the sales managers can see the sales floor and the lot.

43. **Up** - An unattended customer who is in the lot or on the showroom floor.

44. **Upsell** - To sell the customer more than needed. To sell more parts or service on a particular job. To upsell products.

45. **Upside-down** - To owe more money on a vehicle than what is actually worth.

46. **Example**: Your car has been appraised for $12,000. You still owe $18,000 on the loan. You are $6,000 upside-down.

30 Years of Thank You's

I have been threatening to write this book for years. So I have a long list of people to thank for helping me get this far.

Let's start with my wonderful sister, Wendy. She was the catalyst who made this happen. I knew what I wanted to say, but I didn't know how to make it a reality. Then, what do you know? Wendy writes and publishes her own book. I was so proud, yet envious of her. Wendy, you are the happiest and most positive person. Thank you for your insight, and for helping me to bring this book from inside my head to the Internet and on paper. I love you.

Over 30 years ago, at a bachelor party, I met a new friend. He saw something in me that I didn't know was there. He saw through the alcohol. He went out of the box and took me under his wing. He took me to Anders Men's Wearhouse and bought me that first polyester three-piece suit. He offered to buy me food for a month. A few years later he was not only the best man at my wedding, but he was also my best friend. Scott, I'll never forget all the great things that you have done for me and my family. You truly are one of the good guys. Thank you for everything, Scott.

I have been very fortunate in my life to be able to call so many people my friend. Some, of course, are closer than others. But to me, my mother was always and remains one of my closest friends. Even though I didn't become a doctor as she had hoped for, she always believed in me, and always loved me.

No matter what the circumstances were. And there were some circumstances. She has always looked and acted much younger than she is. We have even been mistaken for brother and sister. We always laugh and have fun together. Like the time we went skiing, and I was having so much fun that I forgot that I was with my mother. That's when the chair lift operator asked if we were enjoying our day on the slopes. I looked at him and immediately said, "Fucking A!" I can't thank you enough for everything you have done for me. I love you, Mom.

My son, Bennett. What can I say? I love you, man. I'm so happy for you and Drew. Congratulations on your marriage. Thank you for trying the car business. It really isn't for everyone, is it? But everyone who met you while you were in it, loved you. You have a way about you that is warming and respectable.

That short time you spent in the business with me helped us understand each other. I have always been able to bounce things off of you. Because of that, you get it, and you get me. You don't know how big of a help you've been to me. Bennett, I'm so very proud of you and Buddy, I really love you.

There are a lot of really good managers working the desk at car dealerships. There are so many of you that I could thank right here. I don't want to miss anyone because, so many of you, in one way or another, helped me in learning and getting to where I am in the car business. I owe a big thank you to all of you.

There is one manager that loved his Saturday morning meetings. This guy was an out-of-the-box thinker. He would come up with the greatest ideas on how to motivate the salespeople. He could also motivate his managers. I'll never forget the time that I couldn't close this one couple. He kept sending me down, and I couldn't get them to buy the car for anything. So he thought about it for a minute, and finally, he said, "Rick, you forgot to say *please*. Go back, apologize to them and say *please*." I trusted this guy explicitly. I went back to the customer and apologized and then asked, "Would you *please* buy the car?" And they actually did. To this day we still laugh about that. Jim Omeara, you were way ahead of your time. You are the best. Thank you for all that you have taught me and for the way that only you could motivate me to be even better.

Like salespeople and managers, there were good and bad dealers and dealerships. Two of the best that I worked for were Bill Kidd's Toyota Volvo and Bob Bell Automotive. Both are clearly named after their owners, but what people can't see is that both Mr. Bell and Mr. Kidd were two of the most honest and forward-thinking dealers around. They realized early on that if they took care of their employees, that in turn their customers would be taken care of. Both of these outstanding dealers loved and respected their employees as much as their customers. It truly was an honor to work for such great owners. Thank you both for all that you taught me about not only the car business but also about life. Thank you for the countless opportunities that you have made possible for me.

To Mr. Bill Kidd Sr., and Mr. Bob Bell, may you both rest in peace. I will always remember and love you.

My daughter, Lindsay. Who knew? I thought when this kid was born that she was going to hate me when she grew up. I wasn't going to allow her to go out or date or anything. Turns out, 29 years later, we are best friends. Lindsay, thank you for everything. Thank you for pursuing your dreams and allowing me to accompany you on the way. To say that I am proud of you for pursuing your dreams would be an understatement. To say that this book would never have happened without you and your help is a true statement. I can't thank you enough for doing the first edit. I can't thank you enough for pushing me. I loved when you finished editing a chapter you would text me and asked if I had finished the next one. That really lit a fire under me to get it finished. I love you kid, 88, 10, 13.

Who am I forgetting? Oh yeah, Laura. My beautiful, gorgeous wife. There are no words that I could say to describe how lucky I am. No words could describe how this book doesn't happen without you. Where we are doesn't happen without you.

Five years ago I knew, that when you walked into my office at Bob Bell Hyundai, and reached out and shook my hand, that I wanted to spend the rest my life with you. Little did I know then that you have as well had 30 years in the car business. From the receptionist, to general manager. Wow, honey, that's so impressive. That has helped and will continue to strengthen our relationship. You understand the ups and downs, the ins and outs of the car business. This will keep us together forever.

Laura, I could never thank you enough. I can only promise that I will spend the rest of my life showing you how much I love you. With all my heart I love you.

Together, we are invincible.

Made in United States
Orlando, FL
16 November 2022

24615570R00065